Mind-Bending
Lateral & Logic Puzzles

Editor: Colleen Collier
Puzzle Compilators: Lloyd King, Stan Clarke
Additional Contributors: Peter Sorenti,
Jane Purcell, Belinda Nowland, Sue Curran
Page layout & Design: Linley Clode
Cover design: Gary Inwood Studios

Published by:
LAGOON BOOKS
PO BOX 311, KT2 5QW, UK
PO Box 990676, Boston, MA 02199, USA

www.lagoongames.com

ISBN 1-902813-50-2

Mind-Bending
Lateral & Logic Puzzles

LAGOON
BOOKS

INTRODUCTION

This mind-bending 'Lateral & Logic' book takes puzzling to a whole new dimension.

All the Mind-Bending puzzle books have been carefully compiled to give the reader a refreshingly wide range of challenges, some requiring only a small leap of perception, others deep and detailed thought. All the books share an eye-catching and distinctive style that presents each problem in an appealing and intriguing way. And this one is not only crammed full of some of the best new puzzles ever, but the type of puzzles have been cunningly mixed-up so that you need to be able to switch your brain from thinking logically to thinking laterally with the turn of every page.

Go ahead and try a few. It's the ultimate cerebral workout!

A master of illusion bets you can't figure out his puzzle. He says, "Picture A shows Polly parrot in her cage. Where's Polly gone in Picture B?"

A

B

A young woman is found dead on an island with no food, water, or possessions. She didn't starve to death or die from ill-health, so what could have killed her?

SPECTATORS' ROAR HELPS U.S.A. JOCKEY IN KENTUCKY DERBY

Three letters, N, E and T, have been removed from this newspaper headline exactly once. Stretch your brain by putting them back in their original positions, none of which are adjacent, to discover the true headline.

A man is organizing a party for all his friends. Realizing he's forgotten to buy the beer, he rushes out leaving several inflated balloons on the floor. When he arrives back, he's amazed to see the balloons floating two inches off the floor. How can this be?

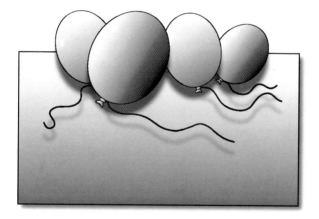

There's a smog-infested city hidden in this picture somewhere. Can you find it?

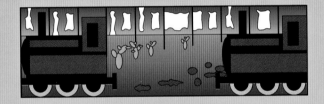

A rogue pilot was about to bomb Germany! The command was given, the hatch was opened and the bomb released. Why didn't it ever hit the ground?

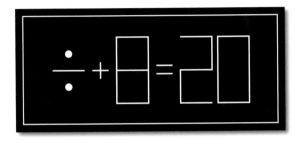

Move one of the two numbers on the right side of this equation to the left side. The answer will make perfect mathematical sense.

A man is discovered dead sitting at his desk, alone in a locked office. He did not commit suicide and there were no weapons in the room. The only clue is a sealed envelope on the desk in front of him. How did he die?

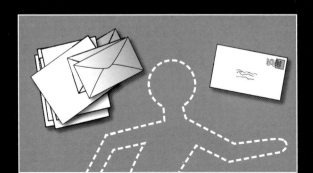

Can you find the six of hearts, diamonds and clubs in this conundrum of cards?

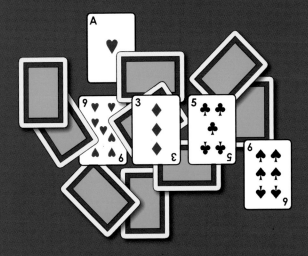

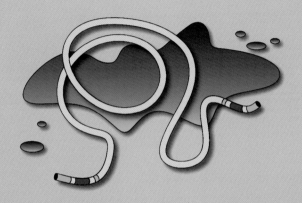

A new Alcatraz for 'lifers' is built in the middle of a vast lake. One morning, it's discovered that a prisoner who can't swim has escaped. The only evidence he leaves behind is a strand of shoelace. How has he done it?

canal

baled

holes

tales

cores

holed

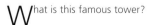

What is this famous tower?

Two men are drinking in a bar. Two women walk in and one man sees them both and says, "I have to go, my wife and daughter are here". The second man also notices both women and says, "I have to go, my wife and daughter are here". Is there a logical explanation for this?

Arrange these seven headless matches to form a single square. None of them may overlap or be broken.

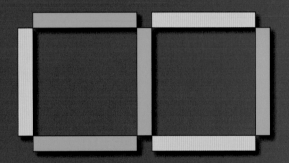

The body of a woman is found in bed. There are no signs of violence and no marks of any kind on her body. The only evidence is a pair of scissors lying next to her. How did she die?

Move only one of these cards to leave a fourth Jack.
Yes, it is possible!

Tracy died in Florida. Shortly after, Craig died at sea. Nobody mourned. In fact, everyone was absolutely delighted. Why?

W hat is the next figure in this sequence?

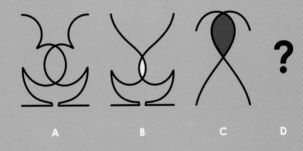

A   B   C   D

There is a line of adults standing with children. Some children are crying, but most are cheerful and happy. At the top of the line, parents willingly hand their children over to a man to be shot, one by one. What's going on?

BCDFGHJL?VWXYZ

What is the only letter of the alphabet not represented here?

A man is replacing the wheel of his car. He suddenly realizes that he has lost the four nuts needed to hold it on. Then a passer-by comes up with a speedy solution that doesn't involve buying more nuts. What is it?

In the following arrangement of fourteen cards, only two cards are spades. There is a way to turn over just three more cards, while leaving at least one other spade showing. How?

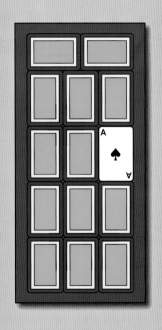

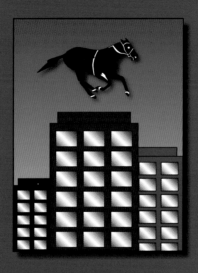

A horse jumps over a tower and the tower disappears. It's not an illusion or a dream so where could this happen?

Rearrange two of these five toothpicks to leave a view of which famous building in the USA?

A Queen has twins by Caesarean section so it's impossible to tell who was born first. Now the twins are adults and ready to rule. One is intensely stupid, while the other is highly intelligent, well loved and charismatic. Yet the unintelligent one is chosen as the next ruler. Why?

W hat seven-letter word can be seen in the middle of this wall?

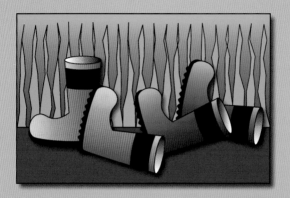

Three men are walking across a green and luscious field. Only two of them are wearing rubber boots and yet the feet of the third man remain dry. Why?

Find another way of arranging the top cube, which has just two letters on its sides, to leave a wise bird facing you.

Jason is lying dead. He has an iron bar across his back and some food lying in front of him. How did Jason meet his sorry end?

By rearranging one of the figures or symbols shown, you can 'thaw' out this mathematical migraine and make sense of the equation. What does it say?

A student zips on his scooter to ride to the train station to get to college. His home is close to two stops; the first one is a mile from home, and the second is two miles from home in the opposite direction. In the morning, he always gets on at the first stop and in the afternoon, he always gets off at the second one. Why?

Can you guess from this picture of a laid table what supper will consist of?

Sally, Lisa and Bernadette are triplets. But Sally and Lisa share something that Bernadette does not. What is it?

A weird and terrible illness has struck in the land of stick people. Only you can save them by putting one of the figures A to E in the space, thus revealing the cause of this mysterious plague.

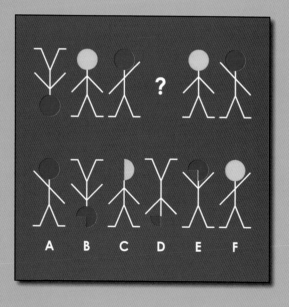

A   B   C   D   E   F

Fred is listening to the radio when it suddenly stops playing. Nobody is with Fred and nobody touches the radio. A few seconds later, the radio resumes playing. How can this be?

	4	5	6	7	8	9	10
M	F	H	✕	S	N	✕	C
N	C	✕	H	T	✕	F	P
O	✕	J	H	✕	C	V	D
P	✕	Y	✕	G	J	O	C
Q	G	H	✕	U	✕	Z	Q
R	✕	D	K	D	K	L	✕
S	T	✕	P	Y	H	✕	N

This map unlocks a big pile of buried treasure, and it also reveals what the treasure is and even what country it can be found in. Can you work it out and claim the gold for yourself?

A man walks into a bar and immediately falls unconscious. Why?

Who murdered Kojak with a poisoned lollipop? Cannon, Columbo, Ironside and Perry Mason are the suspects but the L.A.P.D. are stuck for clues until they receive this anonymous tip off. Which one of the four is the culprit?

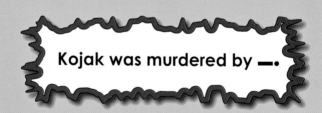

Kojak was murdered by —.

What workers would find their lives a lot easier if they didn't make so much money?

Add two straight lines to this letter 'M' and leave a different letter.

A Californian man with two hobbies decides after much thought to send a letter to a non-existent address. He's perfectly sane so why would he do this?

While on holiday in the USA, I notice this bizarre sign in the hotel lobby. What does it mean?

TORA LEVE

A man sails off on a cruise between Mexico and the USA. He does not stop at any ports and does not even come out of the cabin, yet he makes $300,000 from the trip. How?

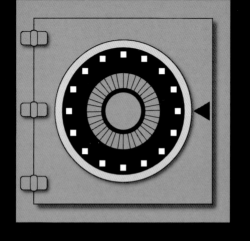

Practice your skills as a master thief. Turn the dial on this safe 180 degrees clockwise, then 90 degrees counterclockwise, and then 45 degrees clockwise, to reveal a single item of jewelry.

A man hurries into a bank one day wearing a mask over his face. The staff notices him but are not at all alarmed. Why?

W hich of the following pictures of the sun, moon, and stars is the odd one out?

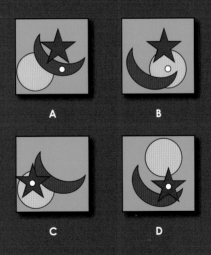

A

B

C

D

Monica took part in a furiously competitive race, which she won due to her speed and agility. Despite this, she was not allowed to collect the winning trophy. Why?

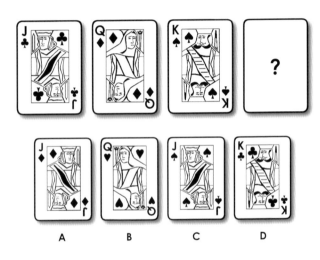

A B C D

Pick one of the four cards labelled A, B, C and D, to be the next card in this sequence.

switches outside a windowless room are
connected to three light bulbs inside the room
determine which switch is connected to
you are only allowed to enter the room on

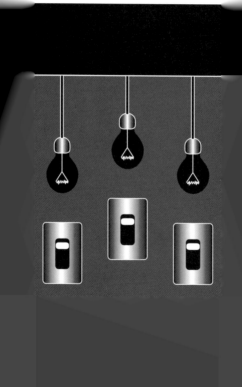

Create some alphabetical angst by arranging these four shapes into two capital Hs.

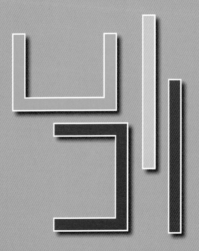

A man buys an expensive item and then loans it to lots of people across the globe. They all use it before handing it back. Why would he be happy about this?

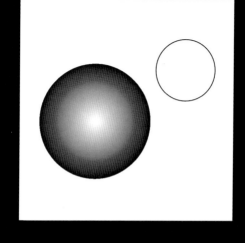

A sphere has three, a circle has two, and a point has zero what?

A man walking along a railroad track sees a train thundering at high speed towards him. Instead of immediately jumping off the track, he charges directly at the train for about ten feet and only then gets off the track. Why?

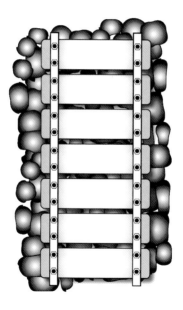

Can you move just two matches to turn this picture of a dog into another dog?

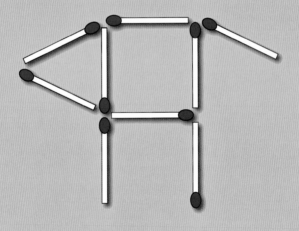

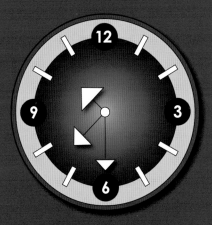

It's Christmas Eve and way past little Holly's bedtime, but she's waiting for the tree to be finished. At exactly what time will this happen?

CON

FIR

MAT

什hat three-letter word can be placed after all these words?

Every time a man strolls past the town hall clock, he sees the same three laborers sweeping around it, however bad the weather or the lateness of the hour. It's neither their job nor or a punishment, and they're not doing it for charity, so why are they doing it?

When you complete the following brain jumble, it has LA on one side and NY on the other. What is it?

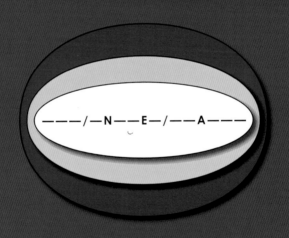

—––/—N——E—/——A———

A certain creature is removed from one continent and moved to the one found on the opposite side of the world. Once there, however, it finds itself back in the one from where it has just been taken. What exactly is this creature, apart from confused?

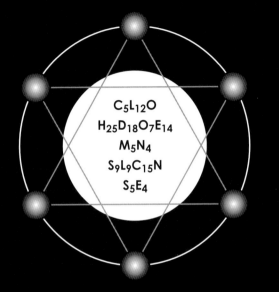

$C_5L_{12}O$
$H_{25}D_{18}O_7E_{14}$
M_5N_4
$S_9L_9C_{15}N$
S_5E_4

Which one of these chemical conundrums is a gas?

A man in a suit steps on a train and, immediately, a woman in a white dress shouts, "Get off!" Why?

W hat single thing about this picture defies all natural laws?

A sleeping passenger on a speeding train wakes to find that it's pitch-black outside. This regular passenger then realizes exactly where she is on her journey. How could she know?

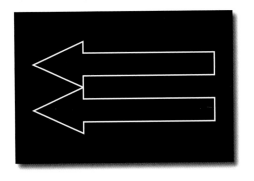

Can you create a third arrow by drawing just two straight lines?

A man pays to cross the river by ferry. One day, his friend also crosses the river, except that he is paid money to cross. Why would that be?

Can you join these five pieces of chain into one continuous length, using a maximum of six moves? To open a piece of the chain is one move, and to close it is another move.

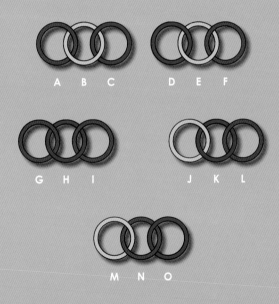

A B C   D E F

G H I   J K L

M N O

S oap operas can be real to the audience, but they can be equally real to the cast and crew on location. During the filming of a high street scene, the crew saw something that completely shattered their efforts at reality. What was it?

If it is 1,800 kilometers to America, 1,200 kilometers to Japan, 2,400 kilometers to New Zealand, and 1,400 kilometers to Brazil – how far away is Morocco?

Riding home one evening, a horseman tumbles into a ditch and bumps his head. The man is uninjured but when he crawls out, his horse is nowhere to be seen. Staggering home where he lives alone, he finds his horse in a locked stable, with the saddle and harness put away. What's going on?

The following numbers have something in common. From the options A, B, and C, what will the next one in the sequence be?

3 7 10 11 ?

4 12 16

A   B   C

A man is working hard when he recognizes an old friend approaching him. Despite both men being fit and well, they cannot speak and have to use hand movements to communicate. Why is this?

1, 13, 16, 61, ?, 217

What is the missing number in this cryptic sequence?

A man is found dead on the floor of his remote cottage, telephone in hand. The policeman who found him walks outside to the hillside garden and finds a three-foot piece of timber in the grass. He suddenly realizes that the timber indirectly caused the man's death. How could this be?

M ove one of these planks to leave more than three but less than four. Yes, you did read the instruction correctly!

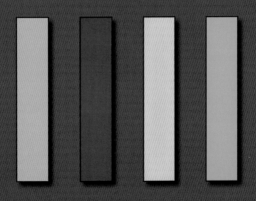

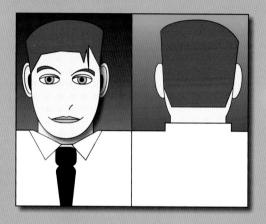

A man goes to work at the same time each day and travels part of his journey facing forwards and the remainder facing backwards. When he returns at the end of his working day, he only faces forwards. How can this be?

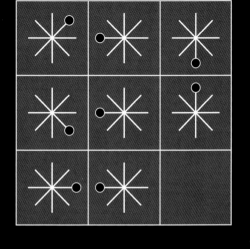

Figure this conundrum out and you can fill in the missing figure in the empty box.

During a soccer match, a player makes a suggestive comment about women into the referee's ear, who promptly waves the red card and sends the player off. Why would the referee do this?

W hat is the next figure in this sequence? Choose from the following four options.

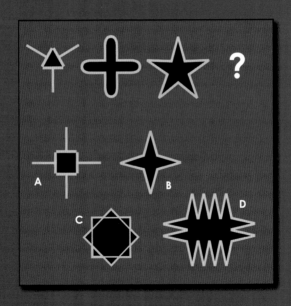

A

B

C

D

George was cleaning the windows on the eighteenth floor of an office block when there was a massive power failure. The electric hoist on his platform was immobilized, so how did he manage to get down before the power was restored?

C an you place the black dot in the correct position in
  this number?

A man strolls into a hospital emergency room where there is a long line up to the reception desk. He walks right to the front and calmly asks to see the consultant in charge. No one gets angry and the receptionist immediately phones. The consultant has never met this man, yet she hurries away from the ward to see him. Why?

SOLUTIONS

Page 6

At the bottom of the cage! The master of illusion actually asks, "Where's polygon in Picture B?"

Page 7

She was run over while standing on a traffic island.

Page 8

Replace the dots in 'U.S.A.' to leave the word 'unseat'. The new headline now reads 'Spectators' roar helps unseat jockey in Kentucky Derby'.

Page 9

A pipe had burst and flooded the living room and the balloons were floating on top of the water.

Page 10

Rotate the picture ninety degrees counterclockwise to find 'Los Angeles' when you read downwards in the sky.

Page 11

The plane was flying upside down!

Page 12

By moving the 'O', there are now two dominoes shown on the left side of the equation and the sum of their spots is two.

Page 13

The envelope glue was poisoned and when the man licked the envelope to seal it, he died.

Page 14

The word 'Six' can be seen on the nine of hearts, three of diamonds and five of clubs in the middle of the arrangement of cards.

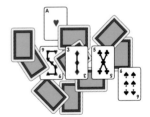

Page 15

The lake is frozen over and the criminal whizzes to freedom on ice skates, one of which has a broken lace.

Page 16

The Eiffel Tower. Each word in the list becomes a letter when rotated ninety degrees clockwise. The letters then spell out the word 'Eiffel'.

Page 17

The two men are widowers and had subsequently married each other's daughter.

Page 18

Page 19

She had drowned. The woman was found on a waterbed that had been punctured by scissors while she slept.

Page 20

Place the King over the right side of the Q on the Queen to leave the letter C. The letters on the last four cards then spell 'Jack'.

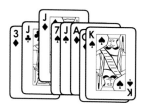

Page 21

They were both cyclones.

Page 22

Each figure is made up of a playing card symbol with its left and right halves slightly overlapping. So the next figure in the sequence is...

Page 23

The children are lining up with their parents to have their photo taken with Santa Claus.

Page 24

The answer is 'P', because the other missing letters – Q, U, E, S, T, I, O, N, M, A, R and K – are represented by the question mark.

Page 25

Use a nut from each of the three good wheels to attach the new wheel.

Page 26

Turn over the three cards indicated to create a picture of a garden spade.

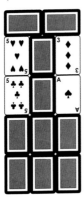

Page 27

On a chessboard.

Page 28

By moving the two vertical matches, you can create a splendid aerial view of the Pentagon.

Page 29

He is male.

Page 30

The white lines in the brickwork between the blue and black lines form the word 'illicit'.

Page 31

The ground is not wet!

Page 32

If you turn the top cube 90 degrees clockwise and then 45 degrees counterclockwise, a picture of an owl appears.

SOLUTIONS

Page 35

The stations and his home are on a hill, which allows him to ride down easily on his scooter.

Page 36

Potatoes (pot and eight 'O's).

Page 37

The letter 'L' in their names.

Page 38

By inserting stick figure C, 'Voodoo' is spelt out by their heads and legs.

Page 33

He is a mouse caught in a mousetrap.

Page 34

By moving the division sign on the right of the equation to the left, the left side can now be interpreted as 'dot, dot, dot' then 'dash, dash, dash,' then 'dot, dot, dot' again. This is the distress signal 'SOS' in Morse code, which can now be clearly seen on the right.

Page 39

Fred was driving his car through a tunnel.

Page 40

The X in square Q8 (Kuwait) points to the letters G, O, L and D (Gold) in diagonally adjacent squares.

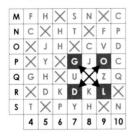

Page 41

It was an iron bar!

Page 42

The 'i on its side' at the end of the message implicates 'Ironside'.

Page 43

Workers at a Mint producing money for the government.

Page 44

Page 45

The man is both a stamp collector and an Elvis Presley fan. The US Government issue an Elvis Presley commemorative stamp, which the man realizes will be much more valuable with a 'Return to Sender' stamp on the envelope.

Page 46

'Tora Leve' is an anagram of 'Elevator', so the sign means 'Elevator out of order'.

Page 47

He is a smuggler.

Page 48

The jewelry is a diamond ring. After the last turn of 45 degrees, the squares on the dial become a ring of diamonds.

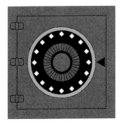

Page 49

He is the manager wearing an anti-smog protective mask after cycling to work.

Page 50

The answer is C. In all the others, the black spot is in exactly the same position each time in the box.

Page 51

Monica is the name of the horse that won the race.

Page 52

The answer is A. The figures' heads on the cards alternately turn to face one side and then the other.

Page 53

Switch the first light on, leave for a minute, and then switch off again. Then switch the second bulb on and enter the room. The recently turned-off light bulb will still be warm, the second one will be on, and the third one will be off and cold.

Page 54

The lines between the pieces form the second capital H.

Page 55

Because he has handed people his camera to take pictures of himself.

Page 56

Dimensions.

Page 57

The man was on a bridge when he first saw the train so he couldn't jump off the track immediately.

Page 58

SOLUTIONS

Page 59

The hands of the clock form a complete Christmas tree at midnight.

Page 60

The answer is 'ion' which results in the word 'Con-fir-mat-ion'.

Page 61

The laborers are the hands on the town hall clock.

Page 62

The United States.

Page 63

The creature is an ant. The ant is removed from ANTARTIC and then added to ARCTIC to leave ANTARCTIC, which is where it started.

Page 64

The answer is $H_{25}D_{18}O_7E_{14}$. If you substitute each number for the letter occupying the same numerical position in the alphabet, you get 'Hydrogen'.

Page 65

The man is a bridegroom and he has stepped on the train of his bride's wedding dress.

Page 66

The flag is blowing the wrong way!

Page 67

Because there is no light outside the window, she knows she must be in the only tunnel *en route* to her destination.

Page 68

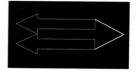

Page 69

The friend is a tightrope walker, and is hired to cross the river by high wire.

Page 70

Open up pieces A, B and C, and use them to attach the other pieces (at DG, IL and JM). The total number of moves used is six.

Page 71

They were filming a scene outside the local TV store when their own program came onto the screens of the TVs in the windows, and wrecked the illusion of reality.

Page 72

The answer is 1,700 kilometers, as vowels in the countries' names are worth 300 kilometers and the consonants are worth 200 kilometers.

Page 73

He may have been a horseman, but that evening he was riding his bicycle.

Page 74

The answer is B. The only vowel each number contains when spelt out is the letter 'E', and so 12 must be next in the sequence.

Page 75

They are both scuba divers on a scientific expedition.

Page 76

128, because the differences between the numbers form the series 1, 2, 3, 4…

12   3   45   67   89

1, 13, 16, 61, 128, 217

Page 77

The man had suffered a heart attack and phoned for an ambulance. But because he lived on a hill, the house name sign in his front garden had fallen down and the paramedics couldn't find him to save him.

Page 78

By placing one plank across the top of the others, you can create the Pi symbol in the spaces between the planks. Pi represents the value 3.14, which is more than three but less than four.

Page 79

He works in the engine room of a liner! To get to work, he walks along the decks from his cabin facing forwards, and down the ladders between decks facing backwards. However, when he finishes, he only needs to face forwards to climb the ladders again and walk along the deck back to his cabin.

Page 80

Each spot on each figure gives a direction. The top row therefore spells NE-W-S, the middle row spells SE-W-N, and the bottom row spells E-W-E. The missing figure is therefore...

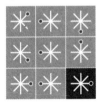

Page 81

The referee was a woman.

Page 82

The answer is D, because the first figure contains three Ts, the second figure contains four Us, the third figure contains five Vs, so the fourth figure should contain six Ws.

Page 83

George walked down the stairs. He was cleaning the inside of the windows.

Page 84

If you turn the numbers the other way up, the word 'eight' is visible, therefore the 'spot' is actually the dot of the letter 'i' in 'eight'.

Page 85

The man is a florist delivering a bouquet of flowers for the consultant.

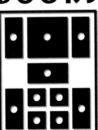